FITBIT VERSA 2 USER MANUAL

The Beginner's Guide to Operate Your Smartwatch Like A Pro

Tech Reviewer

Copyright @ 2019

TABLE OF CONTENT

How to Use this Book 9

Introduction 10

Refined design 11

Always-on AMOLED Display 11

Alexa on the Versa 2 12

Tracking Your Activity 12

Sleep Tracking 12

Female Health Tracking 13

Music on the Versa 2 13

GPS/navigation system 14

Battery Life 14

Fitbit Premium 14

Apps 15

Integration with Your Smartphone 15

Fitbit Pay 15

Chapter 1: Getting Started 16

What is in the Box 16

How to Setup Your Watch 16

How to Set up a Fitbit Account with your Android/iPhone 17

How to Set Up a Fitbit Versa Account on your Windows 10 PC 18

How to Charge the Smartwatch 19

How to Connect your Watch to Wi-fi 20

How to See Your Data in the Fitbit App 21

How to Wear the Versa 2 21

Hand Placement (dominant & nondominant Hand) 22

How to Change Versa 2 wristband 22

Restart, Update and Erase 23

How to Restart Versa 24

How to Turn Off Versa 2 24

How to Turn on Versa 2 24

How to Erase Versa 24

How to Update Versa 25

Chapter 2: Navigation Guide 26

How to Navigate through your Versa 2 Smartwatch 26

How to Turn on the Screen 26

Home Screen and Basic Navigation Shortcuts. 26

Notification/Music controls/Fitbit Pay/Quick settings Shortcut 27

Daily Stats/Apps shortcuts 27

Button shortcut 27

How to Check Battery Status 28

How to Setup Device Lock 28

How to Change Device Lock Settings 29

How to Reset/ Change PIN code on your Watch 30

How to Unlock your Fitbit Device with your Phone 30

How to Activate Always-On -Display Feature 31

How to Adjust Settings on Always-On -Display 31

How to Adjust Screen Wake Setting Directly on the Watch 32

How to Adjust Screen Wake Setting on the Fitbit App .. 33

How to Turn Off the Screen 33

Chapter 3: Fitbit Premium 34

How to Purchase / Start Free Trial of Fitbit Premium 34

How to Start a Fitbit Premium 35

How to See Your Program in a Fitbit Premium Program 35

How to Leave a Fitbit Premium Program 36

Fitbit Premium Insights 36

Fitbit Coach 37

The Fitbit Premium Wellness Report 37

Chapter 4: Clock Faces and Apps 39

How to Change the Clock Face 39

How to Open Apps 39

How to Organize App 40

How to Remove or Uninstall your Apps 40

How to Download Additional Apps 41

How to Update Apps on Your Watch 41

How to Connect your Fitbit Account to an App 42

How to Adjust the Settings of Clock Faces and Apps 43

Chapter 5: Voice Controls 44

How to Set up Alexa 44

How to Interact with Alexa 45

How to Check Reminders, Alarms and Timers Set with Alexa 46

How to Turn Off Alexa Notifications 47

How to Enable More Skills for Alexa on your Watch.......47

Chapter 6: Lifestyle 48

How to Set up the Phillips Hue App 48

How to Adjust Lights from the Watch 48

How to Set up the News App 49

How to Load Starbucks Card into the App 51

How to Remove Starbucks Card from the App................52

How to Set up the Strava App 52

How to Set Up the Uber App 53

How to Request for an Uber Ride 54

How to Set Up the Weather App......................................55

How to Change Units Used for Temperature in the Weather App 55

How to Check the weather 56

How to Add or Remove A City 56

Chapter 7: Notifications 58

How to Set up Notifications 58

How to view Incoming Notifications 59

How to Manage your notifications on the Versa 59

How to Delete a Notification 59

How to Delete All Notifications One Time 60

How to Turn off Notifications 60

How to Turn Off Certain Notifications 60

How to Disable All Notifications; 61

How to reject or Answer Phone Calls 61

How to Respond to Messages 62

How to Customize Quick Replies on Your Versa 2 63

Chapter 8: Timekeeping on Versa 2 65

How to Set Alarm on Your Device 65

How to Dismiss or snooze an alarm. 66

How to Delete or Turn Off Alarms on Versa 2 66

How to Time Events with Stopwatch on Versa 2 66

How to Keep Track of Elapsed Tim with the Countdown Timer 67

Chapter 9: Tracking your Activities and Sleep on Versa 2 68

How to check your stats 68

How to track your sleep using the Versa 68

How to View Your Sleep Data in the App 68

How is the Sleep Time Calculated in the App? 69

How Does the Watch Automatically Detect Sleep? 70

How to Change Sleep Goal in the Fitbit App 70

How to Manage Sleep Insights in the Fitbit App 71

How to Set Bedtime Reminder 71

How to View Your Heart Rate 72

How to Start Guided Breathing Session 72

Chapter 10: Exercise and Fitness 74

How to Play Music Stored on Your Watch During Workouts 74

How to Automatically Track Your Exercise 75

How to Track and Analyse Exercise with the Exercise app 75

Linking your GPS to your Exercise App 76

How to Track an Exercise 76

How to Customize Your Exercise Settings and Shortcuts 78

How to Reorder or Change the Exercise Shortcuts in the Exercise App 78

How To work out with Fitbit Coach App 79

How to Share your activities 80

How to Track Your Cardio Fitness 80

Chapter 11: Music and Podcasts 81

How to Pair A New Bluetooth Audio Device 81

How to Change Bluetooth Audio Device 82

How to Delete an Audio Device from the Watch 82

How to Download Playlists to Versa 2 82

How to Listen to Podcasts and Music on Versa 2 83

How to Delete or Manage Playlists 84

How to Delete Individual Playlists 84

How to Delete All Music 85

Chapter 12: Fitbit Pay 86

How to Set up Fitbit Pay 86

How to Make Payment with Fitbit Pay 87

How to Change Default Card on your Watch 88

How to Change the Order of the Cards 89

How to View Transactions List on Fitbit Pay 89

How to Delete a Card from Fitbit Pay 90

How to Suspend a Card from Fitbit Pay 90

Chapter 13: Troubleshooting Tips 92

How to Use this Book

Welcome! Thank you for purchasing this book and trusting us to lead you right in operating your Versa 2 smartwatch. This book has covered every detail and tip you need to know about the Versa watch to get the best from your smartwatch.

To better understand how the book is structured, I would advise you read from page to page after which you can then navigate to particular sections as well as make reference to a topic individually. This book has been written in the simplest form to ensure that every user understands and gets the best out of this book. The table of content is also well outlined to make it easy for you to reference topics as needed at the speed of light.

Thank you.

Introduction

Are you in search of a sleek, light and comfortable smartwatch that helps you keep track of your heartbeats, weight, pulses, menstrual cycle, and other amazing features? Then you should get the Fitbit Versa 2 smartwatch. The Fitbit company launched the Fitbit Versa 2 in September 2019 with new features like an improved screen, Amazon Alexa support, new sleep tracking functions, and longer battery life. These new additions to the Fitbit Versa smartwatch have helped to make it a strong competitor to Apple and Samsung who are currently leading in the smartwatch industry.

Below are some key features included in the Versa 2 Upgrade:

- Spotify premium access
- A sharper AMOLED screen
- Paid subscription service known as Fitbit premium that gives a guided workout and deeper health insights.
- Voice integration with Amazon Alexa support
- Mobile payments by default

- A personal coaching function that would be introduced in 2020

Refined design

The Fitbit Versa 2 comes in the same round square shape as its predecessors. However, there are few modifications like the smaller bezel and the removal of the brand name from the bottom bezel. It comes in same 1.6 inches size to fit on most wrists. While the first Versa comes with 3 buttons, one on the right and 2 on the left, Versa 2 comes with just a single button on the left which serves as both the Back button and the Select button. Every other navigation you need to do can be done on the touch screen.

Always-on AMOLED Display

The AMOLED touch screen is another improvement to the Versa 2 smartwatch. Apart from having a slightly larger screen display of 1.4 inches, it now has the always-on option that displays the date, time and battery life. When on the AMOLED screen, the color is simply white and black. However, you can wake the smartwatch to view the full-screen color.

Alexa on the Versa 2

Having the Alexa voice control feature on the watch is another great addition. Before you can enjoy this feature, you would need to have an activated Alexa account. Now you can use Alexa to control smart home devices, look up the weather, start a Fitbit exercise and even set your timers/ alarms.

Tracking Your Activity

The device is built to automatically record your activities like running, walking and biking. However, to be able to see your statistics in real-time, like distance covered, you would need to explicitly begin recording of one of these activities. While the watch would automatically record your walks, it would however not record a run if you do not have your phone with you as the Run Detect feature is mapped to a phone.

Sleep Tracking

Fitbit introduced the sleep tracking feature to the Versa 2. On one hand, you have the Sleep Score that analyses your sleep data from the previous night and scores it on a scale of 1 to 100. The more the numbers, the better the rest. On the other hand, the Smart Wake feature is used to gently rouse you from bed. To enjoy this feature, you just need to inform your smartwatch your intended wake time. The watch would allow a 30 minutes window around the given time to find the time you are in a lighter sleep cycle before it can wake you. It prods you gently with a buzz on your wrist to alert you from sleep.

Female Health Tracking

This feature enables female users to track their menstrual cycles as well as receive notifications and alerts directly on the watch. This is similar to what we have on the Apple watch.

Music on the Versa 2

This smartwatch allows you to download as much as 300 songs to your smartwatch to playback when offline. Now the Versa 2 has a new Spotify app, available for only the Spotify premium subscribers that you can use to control playbacks on the Spotify app so long as your phone is with you. This is similar to the Samsung Galaxy watch active and the Vivoactive 4.

GPS/navigation system

Unfortunately, the Smartwatch has no inbuilt GPS system which would require you to take your smartphone along with you. But something interesting about the device is that over time, the device takes a record of your tracking routes and saves it

Battery Life

The Smartwatch is powered by a Lithium Polymer battery that guarantees 5 days of battery life for general use and if you always make use of the always-on-display feature, then you get two days battery life which is better than the original Versa watch.

Fitbit Premium

The company has announced a new subscription service that is called the Fitbit Premium which would roll out to all Fitbit devices for a fee of $9.99/month or $79.99/year. This program is built in a way that once you set a goal on your watch, it pulls out the data and gives you customized training programs, more personalized insights into your health and fitness as well as an advanced sleep metrics.

Apps

In the Fitbit app store, you can access about 450 apps as well as over 3700 watch faces. Examples of the available apps include Starbucks, TRX Training, Spotify, Deezer, Yelp, Uber, The New York Times, Walgreens, Flipboard, and Pandora.

Integration with Your Smartphone

Regardless of the operating system of your phone, you can receive notifications on the watch from your smartphone, you can reject or answer phone calls. For users on iOS, you can view text messages and calendar invites, however, you would not be able to respond to them directly from the watch. Android users can compose voice replies using the Versa's microphone.

Fitbit Pay

This app allows you to make payment for items you buy in stores with the watch's NFC chip. The app works with several credit card companies like Capital One and Chase. You can also use it in the London Underground and the New York City subway

Chapter 1: Getting Started

What is in the Box

- Versa Smartwatch with a wristband (the color and material often vary)
- Charging cable.
- Extra Large Wrist band.

How to Setup Your Watch

To get the best experience, it is advisable to download the Fitbit app for Android phones or iPad and iPhone. To create a Fitbit account, you would need to input your weight, height, birthday and sex to enable the watch calculate your stride length as well as estimate basal metabolic rate, distance, and the calories burn. After you must have created an account, your profile picture, first name and initial of your last name would be visible to all users on Fitbit. You can choose to share other information with third party as the remaining information you inputted on setting up the watch would be set to private by default. Ensure to charge the watch fully before use.

- Before you turn on your device for set up, place it in the charging cradle.
- Then turn on the device
- Log in to your Fitbit account or create an account if you do not have one already on your phone, laptop or tablet.
- Connect your watch with the Fitbit account
- Enable the all-day sync feature to have your complete fitness and health data on the app and on your watch.

How to Set up a Fitbit Account with your Android/iPhone

- Download the Fitbit app on Google play store for android users and the Apple App Store for iPhone and iPad users.
- Install the app on your phone.
- And then click on the app to open it.

For users with a registered Fitbit Account

- Log in to your Fitbit account.
- Click on the Today tab .
- Then click on your **profile picture.**

- Lastly, click on **Set Up a Device**

For users without an existing Fitbit Account

- Click on **Join Fitbit**
- Carefully give answers to the series of questions provided.
- Click on Proceed
- Follow the instructions that pop out on the screen in order to connect the smartwatch to your account.

How to Set Up a Fitbit Versa Account on your Windows 10 PC

To open an account on your Windows 10 PC, you need to have a Bluetooth-supporting windows 10 PC.

- Go to your Microsoft Store on your computer.
- Search for the Fitbit App.
- Click on **free** to download.
- Click on Microsoft account
- Sign in if you have previously registered.
- Click on the Sign-up tab and provide all necessary information if you do not have a previously registered account.

How to Charge the Smartwatch

The following are carefully stated tips on how to charge your Versa 2 watch.

- Plug the charging cable into a UL-certified USB wall charger, your computer's USB Port or another low-energy charging device
- Slightly pinch the clip attached to the cradle and then carefully place the watch right in the charging cradle.
- Also, you must ensure that the gold contacts at the back of the watch get in contact with the pins on the cradle.
- If the charger is well fixed, the charging status automatically pops out on the screen of the watch.
- Allow the Smartwatch to charge fully (100%) before using it.
- Double-tap the screen to check the charging status.
- Click on the screen again to use your watch

How to Connect your Watch to Wi-fi

When setting up your watch, you would need to connect it to a strong Wi-Fi network in order to download your apps and favorite playlists from the lists of apps provided in the Fitbit app gallery and also update the watch to the latest OS. Your smartphone, computer or tablet has to be connected to the same network as the watch.

Here, is how to get connected;

- Go to the Fitbit app and click on the Today tab

- Click on your profile picture
- Select your watch tile
- Click on **Wi-Fi settings**
- Tap **Add Network**
- Carefully follow all the instructions on your screen to connect to Wi-fi.
- Once the watch is connected to a Wi-fi network, your watch would automatically start to download apps or new music when you connect it with the charger.

How to See Your Data in the Fitbit App

You need to sync the smartwatch with the Fitbit app to be able to transfer your data to the watch. It is advisable to activate the option for **Keep All-day Sync** so that the smartwatch can periodically sync with the app. To use features like the Amazon Alexa, the All-day sync has to be enabled.

How to Wear the Versa 2

When not exercising, you should wear the smartwatch a finger's width above your wrist bone.

How to Wear the Smartwatch During Exercise

The tips below are important for optimized heart-rate tracking during exercises

- Place the watch at the top of your wrist, usually 2-finger widths to get an improved fit.
- Ensure that the rear of the device gets in contact with your skin.
- Ensure your wristband is tightened when doing your workout and loosened after you are done with your workout.

- The wristband should be closely fitted, but also ensure it is not constricting around your wrist in order to allow the flow of blood.

Hand Placement (dominant & nondominant Hand)

By default, the Versa wrist setting is set to the nondominant hand. For better performance, you have to set whether you would wear your watch on the non-dominant or dominant hand. The dominant hand is the one you use for eating and writing. If you would prefer to wear on the dominant hand, follow the steps below to change the settings.

- Go to the **Today tab**
- Click on your profile picture.
- Then tap on **Versa 2 tile**
- Tap on **Wrist**
- Select **Dominant**.

How to Change Versa 2 wristband

The Versa 2 watch is packaged with a small wristband attached to the watch and an additional large wristband. You can always swap the two wristbands or buy additional accessories from the Fitbit website.

How to remove the wristband;

- Turn the watch to the rear to see the quick-release lever.
- Hold down the quick-release lever.
- Then gently detach the wristband from your watch.
- Move to the side of the wristband you are yet to detach and repeat the same process.

How to attach the wristband

- Hold the band at a 45-degree angle
- Slide the pin into the watch's notch (the pin is the side opposite to the quick-release lever).
- Hold down on the quick-release lever
- Place the other side of your wristband to the watch.
- Ensure that you rightly fixed in the pin for both sides before letting go of the quick-release lever.

Restart, Update and Erase

You may have to restart your smartwatch in order to solve some issues with your watch while you would have to erase the watch when passing the watch to another user. You update your Versa 2 to get the latest Fitbit OS updates.

How to Restart Versa

To restart your Versa 2,

- Hold down the watch's button for approximately 10 seconds. Do not release until the Fitbit logo appears on your screen.

How to Turn Off Versa 2

- Go to the settings app .
- Click on **About**
- Then select **Shutdown.**

How to Turn on Versa 2

- Press the button on the watch to turn on the watch.

How to Erase Versa

You may wish to hand over the watch to a new user. Ensure to erase the watch to clear your personal data before doing so.

- Open the Settings app ⚙.
- Click on **About**
- Then click on **Factory Reset**.

How to Update Versa

In order to get the latest product updates and feature enhancements, endeavor to update your Versa 2 smartwatch.

- You would see a notification on your Fitbit app whenever there are updates for installation.
- After you begin the update, you would see a progress bar on your watch as well as the Fitbit app while the update downloads and installs.
- Ensure to place the phone and watch beside each other during the update.

Note: Before you begin an update, ensure to plug your watch into the charger as the update tends to drain battery.

Chapter 2: Navigation Guide

In this section, you would learn how to set your PIN code, manage settings, navigate your watch screen and lots more.

How to Navigate through your Versa 2 Smartwatch

To navigate on your watch, swipe up and down, side to side or press the single button. To save the watch battery, the screen would always go off when not in use except if the always-on display setting is enabled.

How to Turn on the Screen

- Tap twice on the screen or press any of the side buttons.

Note, the screen goes off automatically when not in use

Home Screen and Basic Navigation Shortcuts.

An understanding of these various navigation shortcuts enables you to have faster and easier navigation around the watch. The home screen is the clock itself.

Notification/Music controls/Fitbit Pay/Quick settings Shortcut

- With your finger, swipe down from the top of the screen to access shortcuts to Alexa, Fitbit Pay, music controls and quick settings.
- You can also swipe down on the home screen to view notifications.

Note: the shortcuts disappear after 2 seconds. You can swipe down to access them again.

Daily Stats/Apps shortcuts

- Swipe left to see the apps on your watch.
- Swipe up to see Fitbit today/ your daily stats.
- Press the back button to return to the clock face or go to the previous screen.

Button shortcut

- For easy and fast access on some certain features on your smartwatch, simply press and hold down the button on your Versa 2 watch.
- When accessing the button shortcut for the first time, you would have to select the function that the button would be used to activate. You can

always change this function by going to the

Settings app on your watch and then click on the option for **Left Button.**

How to Check Battery Status

Follow the steps below to access the battery status of your device.

- Swipe down your screen
- Hold on for 2 seconds in order for the shortcut tray to disappear.
- You would notice the battery status icon at the top left.

Note: When your battery life is less than 24 hours, a red battery indicator would show on the clock face. The battery indicator flashes when the battery life is below 4 hours. Also, your WIFI won't work when the battery life is 25% or less, neither would you be able to update your device.

How to Setup Device Lock

The device lock is used to secure your watch. To do this, first enable device lock from the Fitbit app, you would be required to input a 4-digit PIN each time you need to unlock your watch. If you enabled Fitbit Pay for contactless payments from your watch, it would automatically activate device lock and you would have to set a code. Device lock is only optional if you are not making use of the Fitbit Pay. You can turn on the device lock from the Fitbit app with the steps below

- Go to the Today tab in the Fitbit app.
- Click on your profile picture.
- Select your Versa 2 tile
- Then click on **Device Lock**
- You would see the option to set up a 4-digit PIN code

How to Change Device Lock Settings

- Go to the Today tab in the Fitbit app.
- Click on your profile picture.
- Select your Versa 2 tile
- Then click on **Device Lock**
- Click to modify your device lock settings

How to Reset/ Change PIN code on your Watch

The steps below would show you how to change your PIN code or reset it entirely from the Fitbit app.

- Navigate to the Today tab on the Fitbit app,
- Click on your profile picture
- Tap on the Versa tile
- You would see the option to modify your PIN Code.

How to Unlock your Fitbit Device with your Phone

Once you input an incorrect PIN code up to 10 times, you would need to unlock your smartwatch from the Fitbit app on your phone. Follow the steps below:

- Go to the Fitbit app on your phone
- Navigate to the Today tab on the app
- Click on your profile picture
- Tap on the Versa tile
- Then click on **Device Lock**
- You would see the option to reset your PIN Code.

Please note that after the PIN code has been reset, you would need to re-add your cards to be able to use Fitbit Pay.

How to Activate Always-On -Display Feature

This feature enables your watch to always show at all times even when you are not making use of the screen. You can also set the battery level and your core stats progress to show on the watch screen. Follow the steps below to enable or disable the always-on-display feature:

- Swipe from the top of the watch down
- Click on the quick settings icon .
- On the quick setting screen, click on the always-on-display icon.

Note that this feature would cause the battery of your watch to drain faster. With this feature on, your device battery would last only 2 days.

How to Adjust Settings on Always-On -Display

The steps below would guide you on how to modify what items should show on the always-on-display clock.

The **Always-On -Display** would automatically turn off once your battery gets to critically low.

- Go to the settings app
- Click on **Always-On-Display.**
- Then click on **Customize.**
- Click on **Clock Style,** to select either an analog or digital clock face
- Click on the **Status bar** if you want the battery indicator to appear on the screen.
- Click on **Core Stats** to display your progress on 2 preferred core stats.
- Click on **Off-hours** if you want the display to be disabled at a specified time.

How to Adjust Screen Wake Setting Directly on the Watch

- From the top of the screen, swipe down and then click on the quick settings icon
- On the next screen, click on the **Screen Wake** icon to modify the settings

- If you want the screen to turn on each time you move your wrist, click on the **Screen Wake to Auto** option.
- To manually wake your screen by pressing the button, click on the **Screen Wake to Manual** option.

How to Adjust Screen Wake Setting on the Fitbit App

Follow the steps below to adjust this setting from the Fitbit app on your phone.

- Go to the Fitbit app on your phone
- Navigate to the Today tab on the app
- Click on your profile picture
- Tap on the Versa tile
- Then click on **Quick View** to turn off

How to Turn Off the Screen

When the smartwatch is not in use, briefly use your opposite hand to cover the watch face, turn your wrist away from your body or press the button to turn off the smartwatch's screen. This does not apply if the always-on-display setting is enabled.

Chapter 3: Fitbit Premium

The Fitbit premium is a personalized function in the app that has advanced tools and guided programs that helps you to reach your health goals. The Fitbit Premium helps you to achieve the following:

- Insights on your progress and activity throughout a health program
- A detailed program designed to meet your fitness and health goals
- Step by step workouts with Fitbit coach

How to Purchase / Start Free Trial of Fitbit Premium

For the Fitbit Versa 2 special edition, you would have a 3-month free trial of this program.

- Click on the Discover tab
- Tap **Guided Programs**
- Go through the overview and then select **Get Started.**
- Ensure to read the details of the subscription and then click on the price to see the price in your currency and begin your free trial.

- For purchase, select either the monthly or 1-year subscription option and follow the on-screen instructions to input your payment details.

How to Start a Fitbit Premium

- Click on the Discover tab
- Tap **Guided Programs**
- Select your desired guided program.
- Go through the overview and then select **Get Started.**
- Follow the instructions on the screen to input your details and set your goals.
- You would see a summary of your program plan. Go through it,
- Then click on **Start** to get helpful tips and view your daily progress.

How to See Your Program in a Fitbit Premium Program

- Click on the Today tab
- Then select your program tile.
- You would see your progress for the day.

- to see your progress for previous days of a particular program or have a preview of upcoming goals, click on the desired day of the week from the top of your screen.

How to Leave a Fitbit Premium Program

- Click on the Today tab
- Then select your program tile.
- Click on the 3 dots at the top of your screen
- Then select **Quit Program**
- Click on **Yes** to confirm your action

Note: it's important to note that your Fitbit Premium programs would end automatically if you are inactive for up to 10 days.

Fitbit Premium Insights

This feature makes use of your fitness and health data to give your observations and customized tips that would help you to achieve your goals. While you would get the standard insights in the Fitbit app, the Fitbit premium subscription gives you a more personalized insight. To see your insight, click on the Today tab . It's important to note that you may not always receive new insights for each day.

Fitbit Coach

This function gives you a variety of guided workouts on your Fitbit watch or on your phone for all fitness levels. As you provide feedback on exercises into the Fitbit coach, the app automatically modifies the intensity and difficulty of the future workouts. To begin, download the Fitbit Coach app from the app store.

The Fitbit Premium Wellness Report

This feature is currently available to select regions and would be available to more regions soon. The wellness report gives you your complete Fitbit data covering the last 12 months. You can export the report from the Fitbit app to share with your doctor or to review your data. To be able to generate this report, you would need to have a minimum of 30 days data.

- Go to the Fitbit app
- Click on the Discover tab
- Select **Health & Fitness Stats**
- Then click on **Wellness Reports**.

- After reading the description, click on the **Preview Report**.
- As soon as your report is ready, click on **Request My Report**.
- Fitbit would send the report to your registered email. Download and save the report.

Chapter 4: Clock Faces and Apps

The Clock Gallery and Fitbit App gallery offers clock faces and apps to personalize your Versa 2 watch and meet your timekeeping, fitness, health and every other need.

How to Change the Clock Face

- Go to the Fitbit app on your phone
- Navigate to the Today tab ⬤ on the app
- Click on your profile picture
- Tap on the Versa tile
- Click on **Clock Faces**
- Then click on **All Clocks.**
- Go through the available clock faces. Click on a single clock face to have a detailed view.
- Click on **Select** to include the clock face to your watch

How to Open Apps

- Swipe left on the clock face to view the installed apps on your watch. Click on the app you want to open it.

How to Organize App

The steps below would guide you on how to change the placement of an app on your watch.

- Press and hold an app until it's being highlighted,
- Drag it to your preferred location.

Note: to be sure that the app has been selected, you would see the icon increase in size and the watch would begin to vibrate.

How to Remove or Uninstall your Apps

You can uninstall most apps installed on Versa by doing the following;

- Tap on the Today tab
- Click on your profile picture
- Move to your Versa 2 tile.
- Click on **Apps**.
- From the **My Apps** tab, search for the app you wish to remove. You may have to swipe up to see it.
- Click on the app.
- Then click on **Remove**.

How to Download Additional Apps

You can add new apps to your Versa Watch right from your Fitbit Apps gallery. To do this;

- Go to the Today tab.
- Click on your profile picture
- Click on the Versa tile.
- Tap on **Apps**
- Click on **All Apps.**
- Check on all the available apps.
- Select the app you want to install.
- To add the app to your watch, tap on **install**.

How to Update Apps on Your Watch

If your watch is connected to Wi-fi, it would automatically update the apps once the watch is plugged into a charger. The steps below would show you how to manually check for app updates.

- Hold your watch close to you then go to the Today Tab in the Fitbit app.
- Click on your profile picture
- Select your device image

- Click on **Apps**.
- For apps that have a pending update, you would notice a pink **Update** button beside the app name.
- Click on the button to update the app.

How to Connect your Fitbit Account to an App

Some apps require that you connect or create an account to use their service. If you do not have an account previously, you would have to create one by visiting the company's website or app. The steps below would show you how to connect your account with an installed app.

- Hold your watch close to you then go to the Today Tab in the Fitbit app.
- Click on your profile picture
- Select your device image
- Click on **Apps**.
- Go through the apps for the app you wish to set up its settings.
- Click or tap on the gear icon beside the app

- Follow the instructions on the screen to login to your account.

How to Adjust the Settings of Clock Faces and Apps

Several apps have options to modify the notifications, customize displayed contents as well as allow specified permissions. Note that when you turn off any app permission, it may cause the app not to function again. Follow the steps below to access the settings

- Hold your watch close to you then go to the Today Tab ⊕ in the Fitbit app.
- Click on your profile picture
- Select your device image
- Click on **Clock Faces** or **Apps**.
- Click on the clock face or app that you want to change the settings.
- Click on **Permissions** or **Settings**.
- Click **Back** once the changes have been done.

Chapter 5: Voice Controls

You can set alarms and timers, check the weather, control your smart home devices and perform several other functions just by speaking to your watch.

How to Set up Alexa

- Go to the Today Tab in the Fitbit app.
- Click on your profile picture
- Click on the Versa 2 tile
- Click on **Amazon Alexa**
- Tap **Login with Amazon.**
- Click on **Get Started.**
- You would need to login to your Amazon account or create an account if you do not have an existing one.
- After you must have read what Alexa can do, click on **Close** to go back to your device settings in the Fitbit app.
- Click on the Amazon Alexa tile in the device settings section and modify your settings if you want to disconnect your Amazon account or modify the language for Alexa.

How to Interact with Alexa

- The first step is to activate Alexa. If you set the button shortcut on your watch to use for Alexa, hold the button for approximately 2 seconds. However, if the button wasn't set for Alexa, swipe down from the top and click on the Alexa icon ◯. The Fitbit app needs to be launched on your phone at this time.
- Tell Alexa your request. You do not need to call out **Alexa** before making your request.

Note: saying the word **Alexa** would not automatically activate Alexa on your smartwatch, you would need to launch Alexa from the shortcut button or the Alexa icon before this can work. The Alexa microphone goes off once you turn off your watch screen or close Alexa. For more productivity, download the Amazon Alexa app to your connected smartphone. Versa 2 has no speaker so you may not hear Alexa's response but can be displayed as text.

How to Check Reminders, Alarms and Timers Set with Alexa

- The first step is to activate Alexa. If you set the button shortcut on your watch to use for Alexa, hold the button for approximately 2 seconds. However, if the button wasn't set for Alexa, swipe down from the top and click on the Alexa icon ◯. The Fitbit app needs to be launched on your phone at this time.

- Click on the Alerts icon ⏲ located at the top right of the screen.

- Then swipe right or left to navigate between reminders, alarms, and timers.

- Click on an alarm to enable or disable.

- To cancel or adjust a timer or reminder, click on the Alexa icon and speak ◉ your request.

Note: Timers and Alarms set in Alexa are different from the ones done in the Timer's app ⏱ or Alarms App 🕐

How to Turn Off Alexa Notifications

- Go to the settings app and click on **Alexa**
- Click on the option for **Do Not Disturb** to enable or disable Alexa notifications.

How to Enable More Skills for Alexa on your Watch

To get more functionality, ensure to install the Amazon Alexa app on your connected smartphone. The app gives you access to extra Alexa skills. However, not all the skills can work with the Versa 2 as only the skills that can convert feedback into text on your watch screen can be used.

Chapter 6: Lifestyle

How to Set up the Phillips Hue App

You can control your smart lights with your Fitbit watch through the Philips Hue system on the watch. The Hue system and your phone has to be connected to the same Wi-fi network while the watch is kept within Bluetooth range of the phone.

- Launch the Philips Hue app hue on your watch.
- The app would begin to look for your Hue bridge.
- You would then receive a prompt on your watch to press the pairing button on your bridge to finish the pairing process.

How to Adjust Lights from the Watch

- Launch the Philips Hue app hue on your watch.
- Go to the Room screen and click on **Off** or **On** to adjust the lights in selected rooms. You have 10 rooms listed in the app; however, you can add the additional rooms in the Philips Hue app on your phone.

- Click on the > beside a room to view the room lights.
- Click on the checkbox beside each light to turn off or on.
- Swipe to the left to access the Scenes screen then click on the scene name to set it.
- Use the Philips Hue app on your phone to rename lights, add new devices, organize the lights and customize scenes in each room.

How to Set up the News App

- Go to the Today tab.
- Click on your profile picture
- Click on your device image.
- Tap on **Apps**
- Click on the gear icon beside **News,** you may have to swipe up to locate the app.
- Click on **Edit Provider List** to adjust the news providers that you can access their articles.
- Then launch the News app on your watch. You can access approximately 10 recent news

articles from the selected providers with the requirements below:

- ✓ Your phone should be close-by with Bluetooth enabled
- ✓ Your phone should be connected to the internet.
- ✓ You have to grant permission to the news app to access the internet and also run in the background.
- ✓ The Fitbit app should be running in the background or foreground of your phone.

- Click on **Filter** to adjust the categories of articles displayed
- Then click on **Done** to save your filters and go back to the list of articles.

The steps below would guide you on how to access app permissions.

- Go to the Today tab.
- Click on your profile picture
- Click on your device image.
- Tap on **Apps**

- Select **News**
- Then click on **Permissions.**

How to Load Starbucks Card into the App

This app is only available in the United States, the United Kingdom, and Canada. Follow the steps below to load your Starbucks card into the app

- Go to the Today tab.
- Click on your profile picture
- Click on your device image.
- Tap on **Apps**
- Click on the gear icon beside **Starbucks Card.,** you may have to swipe up to locate the app.
- Add your Starbucks Rewards program number or Starbucks gift card.
- Ensure to sync your watch so that the card can show in the Starbucks app.
- Launch the Starbucks app on your watch whenever you need to make a purchase, place the watch face close to the reader.

How to Remove Starbucks Card from the App

- Go to the Today tab.
- Click on your profile picture
- Click on your device image.
- Tap on **Apps**
- Click on the gear icon beside **Starbucks Card.**, you may have to swipe up to locate the app.
- Click on the card number.
- Click on the **X** icon beside the number.
- Once the number turns grey, click on **Save**

How to Set up the Strava App

- You can create an account by either going to the Strava.com website or downloading the app on your phone and following the instructions on the screen.

- Go to the Today tab.
- Click on your profile picture
- Click on your device image.
- Tap on **Apps**

- Click on the gear icon ⚙ beside **Strava,** you may have to swipe up to locate the app.
- Click on **Authorize** and proceed with the instructions on your screen to access your account and permit the connection.
- Sync your watch to access recent activities done on the app.

How to Set Up the Uber App

- You can create an account by downloading the Uber app on your phone and following the instructions on the screen.
- Go to the Today tab.
- Click on your profile picture
- Click on your device image.
- Tap on **Apps**
- Click on the gear icon ⚙ beside **Uber,** you may have to swipe up to locate the app.
- Click on **Login** to go to the Uber login page.
- Log in to your account and proceed with the instructions on your screen to access your account and permit the connection.

- From the Uber app on your phone, set your work and/or home address

How to Request for an Uber Ride

- Launch the Uber app on your watch
- The app would use your already set work and home address as your default destination and pickup locations. You can click on the swap icon ⇆ to swipe both pickup and destination.
- You can change the pickup location by clicking on pickup and entering a new address.
- Click on **Confirm** after you must have selected the right destination and pickup.
- You would then see the estimated time of pickup, cost of the trip and estimated arrival time. Move to the right or left to choose a service.
- Click on **Request** to order for a ride.
- Once the driver confirms the ride, you would then be able to see the driver's information. You can cancel the trip or see estimated pickup time by swiping up.

- To rate the driver or change destination address, make use of the Uber app on your phone.

How to Set Up the Weather App

- Go to the Today tab.
- Click on your profile picture
- Click on your device image.
- Tap on **Apps**
- Click on the gear icon beside **Weather,** you may have to swipe up to locate the app.
- The weather app by default shows your current location and this cannot be deleted. You can add additional 2 locations to show in the weather app.
- Sync your smartwatch with the Fitbit app on your phone to have an updated locations list on your device.

How to Change Units Used for Temperature in the Weather App

- Go to the Today tab.
- Click on your profile picture
- Click on your device image.

- Tap on **Apps**
- Click on the gear icon beside **Weather,** you may have to swipe up to locate the app.
- Navigate to the section for Temperature Unit, then click on **Units.**
- Select your preferred unit.
- Sync your device before you launch the weather app on your watch to view the updated units.

How to Check the weather

- Tap to open the Weather app in order to view weather in your current location
- To view the weather in other locations, Swipe to the left.
- Check that your location service is turned on if the weather of your current location fails to appear.

How to Add or Remove A City

- Go to the Today app.
- Tap your profile picture.
- Tap on Versa 2 tile.

- Click on **Apps**.
- Click on the gear icon beside **Weather**.
- To add another two additional locations, click on **Add City**.
- To delete a location, click on **Edit** then click on the **X** icon.
- Sync your device before you launch the weather app on your watch to view the updated locations.

Chapter 7: Notifications

With your Versa 2, you can view text, call, calendar and as well as app notifications from your smartphone. To do this, you must ensure your smartwatch is within 30ft of your smartphone in order to get notifications.

How to Set up Notifications

Before setting up your notification, you must first make sure the Bluetooth on your phone is On and your phone isn't disabled from receiving a notification.

Then set up the notifications;

- Go to Today's tab in the Fitbit app.
- Tap on the profile picture
- Tap on Versa 2 tile.
- Click on **Notifications**.
- Follow the instructions that appear on the screen to pair the watch with your smartphone if you have not paired before.
- To enable notification from apps existing on your phone, like WhatsApp and Fitbit, click on **Add Notifications** and enable the notifications you would like to see. For iPad and iPhone users, the

Versa 2 would show notification from all the synced Calendars to the calendar app while the notification would only show for a selected calendar app for Android phone users.

How to view Incoming Notifications

When you do not activate the Sleep Mode ☾ or Do not disturb ⊖ on your smartwatch, your watch vibrates when there is a notification. You can check unread notifications by swiping down from the top of the screen.

Note, if your watch's battery level is critically low, your Versa 2 won't vibrate when there is a notification.

How to Manage your notifications on the Versa

On your Versa 2 smartwatch, you have 30 notifications after which the new ones would replace the old ones. Follow the steps below to manage your notification.

- Swipe down to view your notifications
- Tap on any notification to expand it.

How to Delete a Notification

- Tap on the notification to expand it

- Then swipe to the bottom and click on **Clear**.

How to Delete All Notifications One Time

- Swipe up to the top of these notifications
- Click on **Clear All**.

How to Turn off Notifications

You can either disable all the notifications in the quick settings or turn off certain notifications in the Fitbit app. Once notifications are disabled, your watch screen would not turn on when a notification hits your phone neither would the watch vibrate.

How to Turn Off Certain Notifications

- Move to the Today tab in the Fitbit app.
- Tap on the profile picture
- Tap on the Versa 2 tile
- Tap on **Notifications**.
- For the notifications you no more want to receive, simply turn them off.
- Then you must sync your watch to save the changes.

How to Disable All Notifications;

- Swipe from the top of the screen downwards.
- Click on the quick settings icon.
- Click on the icon for **Do not disturb**.
- All notifications on your smartwatch would be turned off.

How to reject or Answer Phone Calls

You could reject or accept incoming calls if your Versa 2 smartwatch is paired with the latest operating system for android users and iPhone users. But with an old Android operating system, you can only reject calls using your watch.

To accept a phone call: tap on the icon showing a green phone. Note that the watch only enables you to accept the call but you invariably can't speak to the caller using your watch.

To reject/decline a call: To reject or decline a call using your watch, tap on the icon showing a red phone.

If you have the caller's name saved on your contact list, the name would appear on your watch screen, if not, you would only see the phone number

How to Respond to Messages

Some select apps on your smartwatch allow you to respond to messages from the watch with the pre-set quick replies or you speak your response to the watch. This feature currently applies to watches connected to Android phones. To be able to respond to messages from the watch, your phone needs to be close with the Fitbit app running in the background. Follow the steps below to respond to a message

- Click on the message notification on your watch. Swipe down from the clock face to view recent messages.
- Click on **Reply.** If you do not see this option, it then means that it is not available for the app that sent the notification.
- Choose an emoji by tapping on the emoji icon or select a text reply from the available list of

fast responses. For additional options, you can click on **More Emojis** or **More Replies**.

- For verbal responses, click on the microphone icon and begin to say your message.
- Click on **Send** once done or click on **Retry** to take it again.
- For messages with errors, you can cancel the message by clicking on **Undo** within 3 seconds of sending the message.
- You can change the language that the microphone recognizes by clicking on the 3 dots icon beside **Languages,** then choose your preferred language.

How to Customize Quick Replies on Your Versa 2

Each app gives you 5 default quick text replies. Kindly follow the steps below to change the quick replies:

- Go to Today's tab in the Fitbit app and click on your profile picture.
- Click on the image for your device then select **Notifications.**
- Choose **Quick Replies.**

- Click on the app you want to modify the quick replies for.
- If you want to make the change for all the apps, click on **Default Replies.**
- Click on the reply you wish to change and input your desired text, a maximum of 60 characters.
- Use the back arrow to go back to the list of apps and automatically save your changes.
- Ensure to sync your device so that the new response would show when next you want to respond to a message from your watch.

Chapter 8: Timekeeping on Versa 2

This section includes steps on how to set up your alarm on your Versa watch. You can set up to approximately 8 alarms to occur multiple days in a week or just once. You can also use the countdown timer or stopwatch to time events.

How to Set Alarm on Your Device

- Launch the Alarms app on your Versa 2. You would see the option to set a new alarm as well as the next scheduled alarm on your screen.
- Click on **+ New Alarm.** If you have created multiple alarms already, please swipe up to view this option.
- Click on the time then swipe to set the time for the alarm. Remember to choose either **pm** or **am.**
- Use the back button on your watch then select the days the alarm should be active for.
- Use the back button again to see the set alarms.

   Click on the alarm icon to disable an alarm.

Note: if your battery is less than 8%, the alarm would not go off.

How to Dismiss or snooze an alarm.

To dismiss/disable the alarm,

- Tap the checkmark.

To put the alarm on a snooze mode for 9 minutes,

- Tap the icon 'ZZZ.'

The setup allows you to snooze the alarm as many times as you wish. when you ignore the alarm for more than 1 minute, it would automatically go into snooze mode.

How to Delete or Turn Off Alarms on Versa 2

- To turn off the alarm, Go to the Alarm app on your watch
- Click on the Alarm
- The set the alarm to Off.
- To delete the alarm, tap on the alarm and click on **Remove.** You may have to swipe up to access this function.

How to Time Events with Stopwatch on Versa 2

- Open the timer app on your device.

- If you have previously used the timer, swipe to the right to select the feature for the stopwatch.
- Click on the Play icon to begin the stopwatch.
- Click on the Pause icon to stop
- To reset the stopwatch, click on the reset icon.

How to Keep Track of Elapsed Tim with the Countdown Timer

- Open the timer app on your device.
- If you have previously used the timer, swipe to the right to select the feature for the stopwatch.
- Click on the screen then swipe down or up to set the timer.
- To go back to the countdown screen, click on the back button.
- To start, press the play icon. Once the allotted time is over, your device would vibrate and flash.
- Tap or press the checkmark icon to stop the alert.

Note that you can run timer and stopwatch concurrently.

Chapter 9: Tracking your Activities and Sleep on Versa 2

Several of your activities are being tracked by your Versa 2 watch each time you wear it ranging from your heartbeat rate to your sleep or rest and even down to your hourly/daily activities. Throughout the day, such data automatically syncs with your Fitbit app when it's in a close range.

How to check your stats

- From the clock face, swipe up to access Fitbit Today. The Fitbit Today shows about seven of these stats.

How to track your sleep using the Versa

- Ensure you wear Versa to bed as it automatically covers the time used in sleeping, the time spent in light sleep or deep sleep (sleep stages) and also the quality of your sleep (sleep score).

How to View Your Sleep Data in the App

To see last night's sleep stats in the Fitbit app or on your wrist, you need to sync your Fitbit device every morning. Then click on the sleep tile to access your sleep history. To see specific details for a particular day, click on the desired date. Follow the steps below to see your sleep stats on your wrist

- Endeavor to sync your watch with the Fitbit app when you wake.
- Go to Fitbit Today by swiping up from the clock face.
- Navigate to the sleep tile for your sleep information. You may need to swipe up to access this. If you are unable to find the sleep tile in this view, click on **Settings** at the bottom side of the Fitbit Today and then activate the sleep tile.
- Swipe to the left on the sleep tile to access time spent in each sleep stage, your sleep pattern and your sleep history for the previous week.

Note, you would have to wait a few minutes to determine your sleep stats while the Fitbit app analyses your sleep data.

How is the Sleep Time Calculated in the App?

To get your sleep time, the device subtracts your restless or awake time from the overall time tracked. For instance, if you slept for 7 hours but woke up once for 20 minutes, the time asleep would read as 6 hours 40 minutes.

How Does the Watch Automatically Detect Sleep?

The Versa 2 is designed to automatically detect when you are asleep so long as you wear the watch to bed. If the watch does not detect any movement for about an hour, it assumes that you are asleep. Your device calculates your wake time by your morning movement. So, if you are awake but not moving for a long period of time, your watch could record it as being asleep. You can always delete this log from your history.

How to Change Sleep Goal in the Fitbit App

The time you spend awake on your bed does not count towards your sleep goal, only the time spent sleeping counts. Follow the steps below to change your sleep goal in the app.

- Click on Today's Tab ⁞⁞⁞ in the app
- Then click on the sleep tile
- Click on the gear icon at the top right
- Modify your sleep goal.
- Save once done.

How to Manage Sleep Insights in the Fitbit App

Sleep insight gives you personalized guidance on ways to improve your sleep to achieve a better health system. The more you log your sleep, the more insights you get. This feature is enabled by default. The steps below would show you how to disable it

- Click on Today's Tab in the app
- Then click on the sleep tile
- Click on the gear icon at the top right
- You would see the option for sleep insights. Turn it off.

How to Set Bedtime Reminder

A bedtime reminder helps you to maintain a consistent sleep time. When its time for bed, you would receive a push notification on your connected phone. By default, the bedtime reminder is set to Sunday-Thursday as most people would prefer receiving these reminders on school or work nights. You can edit the schedule to suit your needs

- Click on Today's Tab in the app

- Then click on the sleep tile
- Click on the gear icon at the top right
- Enable the bedtime reminder and choose your frequency and time.

Note: to receive this reminder on your watch, ensure that you have turned on notifications from the app as shown in this book

How to View Your Heart Rate

As you go on with your daily activity, Versa automatically monitors your heart rate.

- From the clock face, swipe up to view your real-time heart rate as well as your heart rate when you are resting.
- When working out, the watch would display your heart-rate zone to help you choose your preferred training intensity.

How to Start Guided Breathing Session

With the Relax app on your Versa 2 device, you would receive personalized guided breathing sessions in a bid to help you achieve moments of calm during the day.

You have the options of a 5-minute session and 2-minute session.

- Go to the Relax App
- The first option is the 2-minute session.
- To disable optional vibration or select the 5-minute session, click on the gear icon ⚙
- Use the watch button to go back to the Relax screen.
- Click on the play icon to begin a session
- Carefully follow all instructions that appear on the screen.
- At the end of the exercise, you would receive a summary on your screen showing how you aligned with the breathing prompts, number of days you finished a guided breathing session in the week and your heart rate when you finished the session and when you started.

Note: You would be unable to pause a session but you can press the back button at any time to quit the session.

Chapter 10: Exercise and Fitness

You can track your workout and exercise using the Exercise app .as well as complete guided workouts using the Fitbit Coach app from the Versa 2 watch directly. Your watch automatically syncs with the Fitbit app and shares your activity with your family and friends as well as show you your overall fitness level when compared with your peers and lots more.

How to Play Music Stored on Your Watch During Workouts

While working out, you can choose to play music from the Pandora app, music app or the Deezer app located on your Versa 2 and even control the music playing on your connected smartphone. To play music saved on your watch,

- Open the desired app.
- Select the music you wish to listen to from the list of songs.
- Get back to the Fitbit coach or Exercise app to begin your workout.

To control music playing when exercising,

- Swipe from the top of your screen down and then click on the music controls icon.

Note: You would need a paired Bluetooth audio device like the speaker or headphone connected to your watch to hear music on your watch.

How to Automatically Track Your Exercise

Your smartwatch automatically recognizes and records several high movement activities that are a minimum of 15 minutes long. Ensure your device is synced in order to view basic stats about your activity in the exercise history.

How to Track and Analyse Exercise with the Exercise app

You can track certain exercises on the Exercise app of your watch to view real-time statistics, which includes calories burned, heart rate data, post-workout summary and elapsed time, all on the watch.

Note: the watch makes use of the GPS sensors of any nearby phone to gather the GPS data.

Linking your GPS to your Exercise App

- Turn on your GPS and Bluetooth on your phone.
- Ensure your phone is paired with your watch.
- Ensure that the Fitbit app has the right permission to use the location services or GPS.
- Crosscheck that the GPS is enabled for the exercise.
  - ✓ Open the Exercise/Coaching App.
  - ✓ Swipe to find the workout you want to track.
  - ✓ Crosscheck that your GPS is turned on by tapping the gear icon. You may need to swipe up to access this option
- Your phone needs to be with you during the exercise.

How to Track an Exercise

- Open the Fitbit exercise app.
- Swipe until you get to the exercise then click on it to select it.
- Click on the play icon to start the exercise or click on the flag icon to set your distance, time or calories goal all dependent on the activity.

- To pause or end the workout, click on the pause icon.
- Click on the play icon to continue with the workout or click on the flag icon to end the exercise.
- You would receive a prompt to confirm that you want to end the exercise.
- You would see a summary of your workout on your screen
- Click on **Done** to close the screen.

Note: On your Versa 2 watch, you would see 3 real-time stats of your preference. Click or swipe the middle stat to show all your real-time stats. You can always modify the stats for all the exercises from settings. If you have an existing exercise goal, your watch would vibrate once you are halfway to achieving the goal and vibrate again when the goal is achieved. If the exercise requires GPS, you would see an icon at the left top when your watch is connecting to the GPS sensors of your phone. When you see "connected" on your screen and your watch vibrates, it means that GPS has been connected.

How to Customize Your Exercise Settings and Shortcuts

You can customize the settings for the different types of exercise on your watch. These settings include GPS, Auto-Pause Automatically. Run Detect Track, Show Laps and Always on Screen. Follow the steps below to do this.

- Open the Exercise app on your watch
- Go to the exercise that you wish to customize.
- Click on the gear icon and navigate through the available settings.
- Click on a setting to modify it.
- Return to the exercise screen when done by pressing the button on the watch.
- Press the play icon to begin the workout.

How to Reorder or Change the Exercise Shortcuts in the Exercise App

- Go to the Today app.
- Tap your profile picture.
- Tap on Versa 2 tile.
- Click on **Exercise Shortcuts**.
- Click on the + icon then choose an exercise to add a new exercise shortcut.

- Swipe left on an exercise shortcut that you wish to remove.
- To rearrange an exercise shortcut, click on **Edit** and then press down on the hamburger icon and pull it down or up.

How To work out with Fitbit Coach App

- Launch the Fitbit Coach app .
- Select your workout. Click on the menu icon at the upper right to preview the workout.
- Click on the play button at the right bottom corner of the screen to start the exercise. You would get a 10-second preview
- Click on the play icon again if you do not want to view the preview. Your watch would vibrate when the exercise starts and when it stops.
- While exercising, click on the Pause button at the right bottom corner of your screen to pause, end your session or skip a move.
- When the session is complete, you would see a summary of your workout that includes average

heart rate, workout duration, calories burned and max heart rate.

How to Share your activities

- At the end of a workout, ensure to sync your watch with the Fitbit app to be able to share stats with family and friends.

How to Track Your Cardio Fitness

- Click on the Today tab in the Fitbit app.
- then click on the heart rate tile.
- You would find a heart rate graph at the top of your screen.
- Swipe on the graph to change it to a cardio fitness graph.
- You would see your cardio fitness level and score.
- For more details, click the arrow at the upper right.

Chapter 11: Music and Podcasts

The Fitbit Versa 2 smartwatch allows you to store your favorite playlists and listen to it with Bluetooth enabled headphones or speakers. Also, you can connect up to eight Bluetooth audio devices to listen to music on your Versa 2. Each time you add a new Bluetooth device, ensure that both your watch and the Bluetooth device are in pairing mode.

How to Pair A New Bluetooth Audio Device

- The first step is to activate pairing mode on the speaker or Bluetooth.
- Go to your watch and launch the **Settings** app.
- Click on Bluetooth.
- Then click on **+ Audio Device.**
- Allow Versa to search for nearby devices.
- The screen shows the list of all nearby Bluetooth audio devices found.
- Tap on the devices you wish to pair with
- Wait for the pairing.

- You would see a checkmark when pairing is successful.

How to Change Bluetooth Audio Device

- Go to your watch and launch the **Settings** app

  ⚙

- Click on Bluetooth.
- Click on the device you wish to use or pair a new device
- Allow some time for the device to connect

How to Delete an Audio Device from the Watch

- Go to your watch and launch the **Settings** app

  ⚙

- Click on **Bluetooth.**
- Navigate down and click on **Remove**
- Select the device you want to delete
- Click on **Yes** to confirm your action.

How to Download Playlists to Versa 2

To be able to download playlists to Versa 2, you would require a computer that has same Wi-Fi Connection with the watch. You would also need to download the Fitbit

Connect app to the computer. Then create a minimum of 1 playlist of podcasts or songs in Windows Media Player or iTunes to download to your watch. For iTunes users, ensure to give permission for the app to share playlist with your watch.

- Launch iTunes on your computer
- Click on **Edit**
- Click on **Preferences**
- Select **Advanced**
- Click on **"Share iTunes Library XML with other applications"**
- Then click on **OK** to confirm

How to Listen to Podcasts and Music on Versa 2

- Download a playlist on your watch
- Connect a Bluetooth audio device to the watch (follow the steps in this guide)
- Launch the Music app on your watch and click on a playlist. If you downloaded several playlists, you may have to scroll to get the desired one.
- Click on a track and then click on the Play button.

- To control volume or change tracks, open the music controls. From anywhere on your screen, hold down on the back button on the Versa 2 and swipe to the screen for Music control directly rather than launching the music app

How to Delete or Manage Playlists

From your computer, you can choose the individual playlists to delete while the Fitbit app on your phone can be used to delete every music on your watch even without Wi-fi connection. You can always add new playlists and delete current ones concurrently.

How to Delete Individual Playlists

- Plug the Versa 2 into its charger
- Launch the Fitbit connect app on your computer
- Then click on **Manage My Music.** Ensure that both the computer and the watch are connected to the same Wi-Fi network.
- Go to your watch and launch the Music app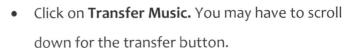
- Click on **Transfer Music.** You may have to scroll down for the transfer button.

- Allow some moments for the watch to connect. Once it connects, you would see a list of downloaded playlists of your watch on the computer screen.
- Tick the checkbox beside each playlist you wish to delete.

How to Delete All Music

- Go to the Today Tab in the Fitbit app.
- Click on your profile picture
- Then select your device image
- Click on **Media**
- Select **Personal Music.**
- Click on **Remove All Personal Music.**

Chapter 12: Fitbit Pay

The smartwatch has a built-in NFC chip that allows you to make purchases with your debit and credit cards on your watch.

How to Set up Fitbit Pay

You would have to add at least a debit or credit card belong to a supporting bank on the Fitbit app to be able to use Fitbit Pay. In the wallet section, you can remove and add payment cards, edit payment methods, set default cards for purchase and review your recent purchases.

- Go to the Today Tab in the Fitbit app.
- Click on your profile picture
- Then select your device image
- Click on **the Wallet tile.**
- Follow the instruction on your screen to add a payment card. Your bank may require further verification. If it is your first time to add a card, you would be prompted to create a 4-digit PIN for your watch.

- After successfully adding a card, you would receive instructions on your screen on how to turn on notifications on your phone if not already done.
- You are allowed to add up to 6 cards to the wallet as well as choose a default payment card.

How to Make Payment with Fitbit Pay

For all customers except for users in Australia

- Launch the Fitbit Pay on your watch. Click the watch button if the Fitbit Pay was set as your button shortcut. If not, swipe down and click on the Fitbit Pay icon
- When prompted, input your PIN code. You would see your default card on the screen.
- To use the default card for payment, position your wrist close to the payment terminal. If you would rather pay with a different card, swipe up on your watch to find the card. Then position your wrist close to the payment terminal.

- For successful payments, your watch would vibrate and you would receive a confirmation on your screen.

For customers in Australia

- when paying with debit or credit card issued by an Australian bank, position your device close to the payment terminal. For cards issued outside Australia or cards not set as default, follow steps 1 to 3 above.
- Input the IN code when prompted.
- For purchases about $100 AU, proceed with the instructions shown on the payment terminal. If you are asked for a PIN at this point, input that of your card and not for the watch.

How to Change Default Card on your Watch

- Go to the Today Tab in the Fitbit app.
- Click on your profile picture
- Then select your device image
- Click on **the Wallet tile.**
- Click on the card you wish to set as default.
- Then click on **Set as Default on Versa 2.**

How to Change the Order of the Cards

- Go to the Today Tab in the Fitbit app.
- Click on your profile picture
- Then select your device image
- Click on **the Wallet tile.**
- Click on **Edit.**
- Hold down on the bars and drag to change the way the cards are ordered. The first card would be set as default.
- Click on **Done.**

How to View Transactions List on Fitbit Pay

Several banks allow you to view the 3 most current transactions you performed with the Fitbit Pay from the wallet section of the app. Follow the steps below

- Go to the Today Tab in the Fitbit app.
- Click on your profile picture
- Then select your device image
- Click on **the Wallet tile.**
- Click on the card and swipe up to view the 3 most current transactions.

How to Delete a Card from Fitbit Pay

When you delete a card from the wallet, the card cannot be used for purchase on your device. You can always add the card again when desired. The steps below would guide you on how to delete a card

- Go to the Today Tab ⁞ in the Fitbit app.
- Click on your profile picture
- Then select your device image
- Click on **the Wallet tile.**
- Click on the card you want to remove
- Then click on **Remove Card.**

How to Suspend a Card from Fitbit Pay

If your device gets missing, you can choose to suspend the linked cards rather than deleting it from the app. A suspended card would stay in your wallet but would not be used for payment. You can always unsuspend the card when ready.

- Go to the Today Tab ⁞ in the Fitbit app.
- Click on your profile picture
- Then select your device image

- Click on **the Wallet tile.**
- Click on the card you want to suspend
- Then click on **Suspend Card.**
- To unsuspend, repeat all the steps and click on **Unsuspend Card.**

Chapter 13: Troubleshooting Tips

Heart-rate signal missing

Your heart rate is continuously tracked by your Versa watch while you go on with your exercises. However, if your heart rate sensor has difficulty in detecting signals as normal, then you can perform the following:

- Navigate to your Setting app.
- Ensure your heart-rate tracking is turned on.
- Check that you are wearing the watch properly, either tighten or loosen the wristband, move the watch lower or higher on the wrist.
- Make sure your Versa is in contact with your skin.
- You should check your heart rate again after your arm has been held still and straight for a short while.

Can't connect to Wi-Fi

If you encounter this problem, it is either that you entered an incorrect password or the password to the connection has been changed. To resolve this issue, do this;

- Go to Today tab .
- Click on your profile picture.
- Tap on Versa 2 tile.
- Click on **Wi-Fi Settings**
- Tap on **Next**.
- Tap the network you want to use.
- Tap on **Remove**.
- Tap **Add Network**
- Carefully follow the instructions that appear on the screen to reconnect the Wi-Fi network.

To ensure that your Wi-Fi network is working perfectly well

- Connect another device to your network
- Make attempts to reconnect your Versa 2 if the new device connects successfully.
- If Versa still won't connect to Wi-Fi, make sure that you are connecting the watch to a compatible network.
- It's advisable you make use of your home Wi-Fi for the best results.

- Once you confirm that the network is compatible, restart your watch and try connecting to Wi-Fi again.
- Place your watch close to your router.

How to Fix Sync Problem on Fitbit Versa 2

Have you made several attempts at syncing your watch with your smartphone or your Windows 10 PC? But the app keeps taking time to complete its syncing or your Fitbit tracker cannot be found. Well, not to worry, the following tips would help you solve this problem.

How to force a manual sync

To force a sync,

- Tap on the member card icon.
- Search for the name of your Fitbit tracker and tab on it,
- Tap on Sync Now.

Usually, Fitbit trackers sync data to smartphones, tablets, and PCs using Bluetooth.

Easy tips in solving Sync problems on your Fitbit Versa

- Frequently update your Fitbit app.

- Only sync your Fitbit to one device.
- Disable Wi-Fi when Bluetooth is on.
- Check the Fitbit battery to ensure that it hasn't run out of power.
- Restart your Fitbit tracker in order to refresh the device's OS.
- Reset your Fitbit tracker.

This only can be used when the sync error still persists.

Tips to Extend Battery Life

- Prevent the screen from coming on every time you move your wrist.
- Do not charge your device in extreme heat or cold.
- Active auto-brightness or dim the screen. From the settings app , click on the brightness settings to change it.
- Disable the always-on display setting.
- Reduce how you use music apps, music control, GPS and Fitbit pay.
- Disable notifications that are not important.

- you may change your clock face as the animated clock faces usually require that you charge frequently.
- Disable some Fitbit devices that you are not using.

Chapter 14: Conclusion

The Fitbit Versa 2 smartwatch offers a lot of features that users would find beneficial like the female health-tracking, insightful sleep tracking, and the improved battery life. Everything you need to know about this smartwatch and how to maximize it has been included in this book to enable you achieve maximum performance from your smartwatch.

If you are pleased with the content of this book, don't forget to recommend this book to a friend.

Thank you.

Made in the USA
Coppell, TX
18 August 2024

36117144R00059